The Art of Negotiation

Introduction

Whenever you want something, either an item or assistance from someone else, the process by which you obtain what you want is a form of bargaining. Therefore, we use bargaining every day in many different situations. Whether you are trying to save some money on a new car, want a better grade in a college class, or are deciding on what to do for a date night, negotiating is involved. Learning to bargain, negotiate, and haggle effectively can save you money, make your life easier, and provide a sense of satisfaction.

The Difference between Negotiating, Haggling, and Bargaining

There are semantic differences between the words negotiate, haggle, and bargain. These three words cause different reactions in most people.

- Bargaining

    When you bargain, you are seeking the best available price. Bargaining involves price comparison. Those who bargain are seeking the biggest and best item for their money. This term is used by stores to indicate they offer the best price and has a positive connotation.

- Negotiation

    Most people think of using negotiation either in conjunction with seeking a beginning salary, or an increase or raise in their pay. A rather "white collar" term, the implication is seeking what an individual feels they deserve.

- Haggling

    Probably the term with the most negative connotation, most people think of haggling as a type of arguing that involves getting an item at a price that may or may not be fair. Haggling is conversational bargaining. It is a duel of words designed to get the best deal for the least amount of money. Frequently, those involved in haggling have no set goal as to the outcome. The most successful haggling leaves both parties with a feeling of satisfaction.

Although the three terms are different and cause a differing emotional reaction when used, they are basically the same. The rules for getting a good deal apply to bargaining, negotiating, and haggling. The purpose of this book is to present the best way to get the best price possible. To do so, we will look and how, when, and where to bargain. We will also provide some quick tips to get you started on the road to getting what you want at the best price possible.

The Art of Negotiation

Table of Contents

Introduction

The Art of Negotiation

Prepare to Negotiate or Bargain

If you are planning on doing business with someone again, don't be too tough in the negotiations. If you're going to skin a cat, don't keep it as a house cat - Marvin S. Levin

In order to negotiate or bargain, you need to take some steps prior to doing so to be effective. Those who prepare for negotiation are not only successful, but also are more likely to get the best bargains.

Do Some Research

To begin with, look for places with bargains. Discount stores, bakery outlets, consignment shops, and yard sales all help you become familiar with local prices and the values available.

Generally speaking, the more information you have, the better you will be able to bargain. Of course, this is not always possible. There are always those spontaneous times when a bargaining situation seems to fall in your lap. However, as a beginning bargainer, take the time to research, especially if you are buying big-ticket items.

When a friend was buying a new car, he noticed there were two dealers located relatively close to each other – within 25 miles. He went on-line and looked at the cars they were offering and wrote down prices and options. Then he chose the dealer with the best ratings and paid them a visit. He bought a car similar to the one he found on-line – different color – but with more options. He used the information from the other dealer in his negotiations for additional upgrades.

Find Out What Locals Pay

In many places where bargaining is common, what the locals pay is usually far less than what a tourist pays. Although you will probably not get as good a deal as you would if you were the seller's relative, with some research and a great deal of patience you may get close. In this situation, it is important to decide how much the item is worth to you. You need to either go with the vendor's best price or be ready to walk away.

Prepare to Spend the Necessary Time

Effective negotiation or bargaining takes time. Sellers are hoping you get impatient and pay what they are asking rather than take a long time haggling with them. Once you prepare to spend the necessary time, relax. The seller will recognize from your body language and attitude that you are into the bargaining process for the long haul, which can serve you well.

Evaluate the Bargaining Situation

Many cultures consider bargaining to be part of the sales process. I have friends that have learned skills while serving in the U.S. Air Force in Thailand.

Not all environments and situations are suitable for bargaining. Know the situations in which it is appropriate to bargain. An outdoor market in a large Asian city may be ideal, but your local high-end clothing store probably is not. We will discuss some specific situations where bargaining worked in an unusual situation later. However, the rule to follow, especially for the beginner, is to make sure you are choosing a venue in which success is not only possible, but also probable. As you hone your negotiating skills, the ability to analyze the bargaining situation will become easier and almost instinctive.

Analyze the Sellers Price

Remember that the seller has set a price to cover his overhead and provide a profit. Approach the bargaining opportunity respectfully, considering all the probably reasons the seller has for setting his price. Basing your bargaining on your analysis of the seller's price will help you start with an offer that is reasonable.

If you are bargaining in an environment where bargaining is a normal part of the selling process, the vendor may have tripled the price anticipating a cut. In this case, you can begin with a lower offer and work from there.

Decide How Much You Are Willing to Pay

Deciding what the item is worth to you before negotiations begin is extremely important. Without this step, one of two things may happen:

1. You will be unhappy about the price you pay.

2. You will end up paying more than you think the item is worth

Either outcome will make your bargaining experience disappointing. If you know up-front how much you are willing to pay, whatever the final price agreed upon, you will walk away pleased with your purchase.

Know Your Break-Even Point

Years ago I worked for a national retailer. At the time my ambition was to become a retail clothing buyer and I was enrolled in a training program. The manager under whom I was working explained that all retail prices are 50% over the cost of the item to pay for the store's help, advertising, and other overhead. A bargain wasn't a bargain unless it was at least 40% off the retail price, preferably less. Unfortunately, that information has stayed with me, making it impossible for me to feel I have a good deal unless I get the item for less than 50% off the original price.

Your break-even point is the amount you are willing to accept before walking away from the negotiation. Setting this amount upfront keeps you from accepting a deal that will present buyer's remorse later.

If you are negotiating a deal for someone else, get their break-even point in writing before you begin to deal. This is especially important for big-ticket items like cars and houses. Even if you are simply negotiating for a friend or spouse, discussing what they expect in the way of a good deal up front avoids disappointment for you both.

Before you begin negotiating or bargaining, do your research and find out what locals pay. Then prepare to spend whatever time is necessary. When you get to the bargaining situation, before you actually start bargaining, take time to evaluate and then analyze the seller's price, remembering your break-even point and how much you are really willing to pay.

Negotiating the Bargain

Money can't buy love, but it improves your bargaining position -
Christopher Marlowe

Once you have taken the steps to prepare for bargaining, it is time to apply what you have learned. The research you have done and the decisions you have made should provide you with the confidence to successfully negotiate a bargain. Read the following for step-by-step assistance in the actual negotiation process.

Take Cash with You

Frequently you want to have cash in hand because it allows you to seek a discount for cash. Many sellers do not like to pay transaction fees for the use of a credit card. Some sellers prefer cash, especially in certain environments, such as discount retailers and flea markets. Some additional benefits of carrying cash are:

- You will not be tempted to buy an item for too much, because you only have a certain amount of cash.

- You can hold out your cash to entice the seller.

Determining Where to Start

Start at 25% to 30% lower than the listed offer or first offer. If you ask for half off the price, you may insult the seller and 10% means you are not getting much of a deal. Of course, this is dependent on the situation and not a hard and fast rule. As you improve your bargaining skills, determining what amount to start your bargaining at will become easier.

Avoid Giving the First Number

Try to get the seller to give the first number. This gives you the information necessary to determine your strategy for moving forward. If the seller's first number is way more than you plan to spend and his body language indicates a lack of desire to bargain, you may decide not to attempt to bargain on price, but concentrate on presenting some other, non-monetary incentive. Also, watch for intonation. Does he state his price as if it is a question? If so, he is probably open to negotiating his starting price.

Negotiating Is Not Always About Money

Remember that we previously mentioned "non-monetary incentives." In any negotiation, there are many intangibles that one or both parties value. Many times, these intangibles are sensed more than spoken.

When our family made a move to North Carolina, we were determined to find enough property that we would have privacy and plenty of room. We found an ideal piece of property. It was 115 acres with a dedicated right of way for a driveway that ran between two neighboring properties, but had no street frontage. The property was perfect for our needs. It had a pond, two streams, and was isolated and private. We made an offer that we were pretty sure was too low, but it was all we could afford. Sure enough, the owner said it just wasn't enough. However, a few days later, she called and said that she didn't know why, but she was motivated to let our family have the property. We are still living there twenty years later and loving it!

Keep Quiet

Never forget the power of silence, that massively disconcerting pause which goes on and on and may at last induce an opponent to babble and backtrack nervously. Lance Morrow

Simply say nothing.

It is human nature to say something when silence continues for longer than about thirty seconds. If you find it difficult to wait, make yourself count silently to 30 before saying anything. You will be surprised how many times the other person comes up with a better offer to fill the silence. Just be careful not to negotiate against yourself if your opponent uses silence on you!

If you simply cannot stay quiet, use noises that indicate you are thinking, such as, "Um," "Let's see," or even, "Let me think about this for just a minute or so."

Be prepared for one of two reactions when you use silence:

1. A bit of rambling to themselves, during which you must not respond, and then another offer

2. Repeating their last offer and possibly asking you to tell them what you think.

Be careful. The seller may use silence on you. Once you have made your offer, do not change it until it is met by a counteroffer. If you are really uncomfortable with the silence, you can repeat your most recent offer and ask if they have any questions. You can also ask for a counteroffer, i.e., "What can *you* offer?"

Learn to "Read" the Seller

You need to pay very close attention to the seller, noting facial expressions, body language, and tone of voice. To do so, ask the seller questions to find out what is important to them and how you can meet their wants and needs.

Sometimes negotiations are unsuccessful because one or both people develop a negative attitude. Make sure you do not let personal reactions sidetrack the negotiation. Try to remain objective, read the seller, and find out what it is they want from the deal. Doing so will help you walk away with a good deal you both feel good about.

Reading the seller also means noting the time, place, and environment in which the deal is negotiated. Use whatever presents itself during the bargaining process. We were seeking to buy a larger car for our family of six. As the kids got older and the legs longer, even a roomy sedan would not suffice. Time was at a premium, so one Friday night after a diner out, when the kids had fought (Again!) over who was sitting where, we headed to the local Toyota dealer. There was a red van and red just happens to be my spouse's favorite color. As luck would have it, we got a young salesperson who obviously thought we were his worst nightmare – a family of six, with dessert-satiated kids on a Friday night when he had a hot date. Needless to say, within a relatively short amount of time, we were out of there with a new van and a fantastic deal.

Be Prepared for Multiple Outcomes

You will be more successful as a negotiator if you do not limit yourself by only considering one possible outcome. Although you may set a desired goal – get new furniture for the home addition you just completed for example– you need to be flexible about how you will achieve that goal. You may get a discount on a full room, or the seller may offer free delivery. Being prepared for multiple outcomes opens up the possibility to get a better deal than you anticipated. When you come to the table with as many different options for success as possible, good deals come faster and easier.

Create a Win, Win Situation

Negotiation is not about winning. It is about reaching a mutually beneficial decision for both parties involved in the negotiation. If you enter negotiations with the attitude that you must "win," you may succeed, but the experience will not be a pleasant one. Additionally, if you set up a "win, lose" situation, you may be the loser!

Now that you know the basic tactics of a good negotiation, it is time to hone that skill and become a "professional" bargainer.

Improving Your Negotiating Skills

My father said: "You must never try to make all the money that's in a deal. Let the other fellow make some money too, because if you have a reputation for always making all the money, you won't have many deals."
- J. Paul Getty

Once you have learned the basics of negotiation, it is time to work at improving your skills, and there is always room for improvement.

Practice, Practice, Practice

You will gain a number of benefits from practicing your negotiating skills, but the primary one is gaining confidence. Begin by asking those you buy from frequently for discounts. When doing retail shopping, try using the following phrases:

- Are you offering any discounts today?

- Oh, my! I wasn't expecting that price!

- That is more than I wanted to pay.

Remember to wait for their response after you use one of these phrases.

Learn to Flinch

Body language is one of the most effective bargaining techniques to master. A visible flinch in reaction to a price makes the seller feel uncomfortable with the price they are asking. A flinch says that you are surprised and shocked by the price and will induce one of the following reactions.

1. The seller will become very uncomfortable and begin rationalizing their price.

2. The seller will offer an immediate concession – a lower price or additional options.

Flinching is natural for some of us – I have never had any trouble with this one. We will talk later about taking a partner along when you negotiate. My role as the partner is to use body language – the flinch, impatience (felt naturally when bargaining goes on and on and the kids are getting restless), and the grimace. If such responses do not come naturally, and they don't quite often, they can be learned. Try standing in front of a mirror and practicing silent reactions to thoughts about a buying experience not going as you had hoped.

Negotiate with the Right Person

Successful negotiators learn to negotiate with the person who is able to give them the best deal. For example, most car dealerships have sales men who show cars, but the sales manager actually reviews the deal and accepts or rejects the offer. Talking extensively to the sales man in an attempt to get a good deal may be a waste of time. Start your negotiation with the sales man, using the information you have gathered in your research, but save your main efforts for when you talk directly to the sales manager.

Years ago, my spouse wanted to buy a second car, one simply to take me to and from work. We wanted something with good gas mileage and a low upfront price. This was over twenty years ago and we chose a Yugo, only $3,000 new. We used to joke that if it broke down, we would simply pick it up and put it out by the curb for the trash man to pick up – it was that lightweight. The local dealer had an advertised special - $3,000, with several attractive options. It was late evening on a Friday when they decided to get to the dealer while they were still open. Only one man was there and he informed that the advertised car was not available.

Well, they are not one to go for the unavailability of an advertised item. He got what was advertised and also managed to get undercoating and upgrade the radio. The man said he would have the car available on Monday. We signed the papers and paid for the car. When we went on Monday, we found out the guy that sold him the car was the owner of the dealership. The sales manager could not believe the deal they'd obtained! He tried to change it, showing the papers indicating the price they paid for the car; they actually did not make any money on that car. So we got the car at the agreed upon price.

In some situations, it is best to ask directly for the manager. As you hone your bargaining skills, you will learn which retailers give discount decisions only to their managers. You may even get to know some of these individuals and gain good deals from them regularly.

Make Friends with Those Able to Give Discounts.

We found a bargain at a local garden center and it just happened that the manager checked us out. We explained we had a very large yard and were in the process of landscaping and needed many plants. After that visit, we would ask to see him and he would look over his stock for plants that needed to be moved out and let us buy them at a reduced price.

Don't Be Intimidated

Remember not to be intimidated by a title. Negotiation is possible in any situation and withy any individual, even a doctor or a lawyer. John Santa, M.D., director of the Consumer Reports Health Ratings Center, says that almost everyone in health care—whether physician's offices, hospitals, or labs – will eventually accept less if you dispute an out-of-pocket charge. He adds that they will try to wait you out, make you feel responsible, and drown you in information. Abbie Leibowitz, M.D., co-founder of Health Advocate, which specializes in health care advocacy and assistance, says his company often cuts charges in half for uninsured patients.

Be Honest and Upfront

Part of negotiation is simply letting others know your honest opinion and what your expectations are. If you get a meal from your favorite restaurant that is not as good as usual, tell your server or even the manager, if you feel it is necessary.

I was visiting my daughter and her family when they were doing some home renovations. The two bathrooms needed new floors and it was reasonable to have the task completed on the same day. The toilets were old and had to be removed professionally, so we ended up with 24 hours

– overnight – with no toilets. We checked into a local motel late in the evening. The next morning my daughter told me that her room had a wet floor and she was having an allergic reaction. I called the motel and told them, explaining I simply wanted to let them know so that they could fix the situation. In response, they gave me a free night's stay.

Determine the Opening Offer Based Upon the Situation

- Think Big

    Be willing to bargain for big bucks. Depending upon the situation, open high at your maximum price. Just remember to make it an amount for which you can argue logically. The primary reason for starting high is that the other party is going to negotiate to a lower level and you want to have a sufficient bargaining range. Remember that you want to be able to make some concessions to your opponent's requests in order to provide them a sense of satisfaction and create that win, win situation.

- Consider an Outrageous Request

    Sometimes it works to use the element of surprise and make a really outrageous request. Of course, this follows your research, the preparation you have made, and should be based upon the knowledge you have of the seller, the product, and the market.

- Offer the Lowest Reasonable Amount

This strategy works if you do not want a counter-offer lower than your first offer. Again, whatever you offer must be based upon a solid foundation of research and preparation.

Take Someone with You

Get a friend, family member, or spouse to work with you. Young, hyper children can be especially effective. A fidgeting sibling or wife/hubby with a bored expression can pave the way to a good deal very quickly. When my sister married, she was embarrassed when her husband asked for a bargain. That discomfort served them well. However, his abilities were so admirable, she decided his was a skill she (and I) needed to learn. No longer were we as effective as bargaining chips.

Don't Take "No" for an Answer

Those new to bargaining frequently make the mistake of thinking "No!" is the end of bargaining when it actually just the beginning. Pretend that "no" is simply "not yet." The timing may not be right, the mood of the seller may be off, or there may be many other unknown factors influencing the bargaining situation.

You don't have to take no for an answer. Some of the methods you can use when a person says, "No!" are:

- Try another time under different circumstances.

- Ask in a different way.

- Ask questions or make conversation to put the seller at ease and then ask again.

Try to add issues that make the negotiation more than just a about the price. If you can make the situation relaxed and friendly, and appeal to the emotional needs of the seller, they are more likely to be open to negotiating.

Anticipate Counter-Offers

Anticipation is an important tool for negotiation, especially when it comes to counter-offers. Make sure you have an adequate comeback for objections. This takes practice, but a few phrases can serve you well:

- "I understand where you are coming from."

- "Well, what is your lowest offer?"

- "I am willing to meet you halfway. How about . . . "

Be Willing to Walk Away

When you know you have reached the end of the negotiation, be ready to walk away. The other party may call you back, if not immediately, a few days later. Just be careful you do not get so involved in the negotiation process that you end up unsatisfied with the result.

Make sure you leave information about how the other party can reach you. You may wish to say something like, "Let me leave you my card in case you wish to contact me."

Offer to Pay Cash Up Front

Sometimes the best negotiation strategy is not to bargain at all. Offering an up-front payment may encourage the seller to provide additional options or a discount. A seller may go for an up-front payment for several reasons:

- You are able to use the set amount you have offered as its own negotiation tool. The seller knows the final amount you are going to offer.

- For a large ticket item (a car, for example), the amount is large enough to be impressive and hard for the seller to resist.

- Cash provides less risk for a seller (bouncing checks, declined credit, etc.).

Offer or Request Extras

Whatever side of the negotiation you are on, see if you can sweeten the deal in any way. Asking for or granting perks or extras is a way to push a deal closer to a satisfactory end. Lots of small incentives can sometimes make it seem as if you are offering more than you actually are.

When buying a car, we always has the tank filled by the dealer. Our reasoning is that they put gas in for you to leave the lot, and it doesn't cost them that much to fill the car completely.

Recognize the Closer

A closer is a fact or argument you can use when you sense the other side is close to a deal but needs that final push. It is important to recognize the closure, or you may miss out on a good deal. Remember that some buyers, such as those looking for a new house, are going to buy and may have a time constraint. Knowing they are going to buy soon and from someone is a good motivator for closing the deal.

Keep a Few Tricks Secret

Always hold back a closer or two. Also, don't project fondness or over-enthusiasm for whatever you're eyeing. As soon as the other party knows how much you like something, they have the upper hand in the negotiation. Keep you desire to obtain the item secret.

Sometimes you can get a better bargain if you choose a time when life's responsibilities are paramount: right before or after lunch or dinner times, close to closing, or on a very slow business day when products are not moving quickly. Try late in the day at outdoor markets and whenever purchasing perishables. Ask the meat or bakery manager to discount products with tomorrow as an expiration date.

Look for Mars and Mistakes

Never hesitate to consider a less than perfect item as a bargain. My daughter found a perfect traveling case for her notebook. The color she wanted did not have a strap attached. She took it to the cashier and they searched together for the strap, taking out the paper with which it was stuffed – no strap. She offered to go ahead and buy it, with a 25% discount. The sales clerk got the approval of her manager and my daughter got her notebook traveling case. Later in the week she was leaving town and packing her laptop. The strap was in a zipper pocket.

I love my gas stove! It is top of the line, a heavy black kitchen dream. It is all the more special because it was purchased at half price! It was a return and has one ding on the front. I also love my refrigerator with an ice maker that makes crushed ice and a large pull out freezer below. I never would have had this luxury model if it had not been the store's display with a price 1/3 off the original because one of the drawers has a tendency to stick.

Beware of the "Final Offer"

A "final offer" is not necessarily final. Of course, if the offer meets your needs, go ahead and accept it. However, the seller may be trying to get you to accept his most recent offer. This "final offer" may simply be the seller trying to let you know they do not want to go any lower. If you decide to counter, offer a reasonable lower increment from which you can both continue to bargain. If the seller's offer was really final, he will let you know at this point.

Concentrate on Success

Statistics show that 89% of those who bargain are rewarded at least once. You will not be successful every time you set out to get a good deal. However, do not get discouraged. You may simply be setting yourself up for failure by not preparing adequately or making some other mistake. Objectively analyze why you are not being successful and make any necessary corrections in your negotiation skills. Then concentrate on your successes. For me, it helps to remember all the times negotiation has resulted in excellent savings for our family. Through the years, we have saved thousands of dollars. Remembering our successes helps keep me looking for those really great bargains.

Bargain on Everything!

Sometimes we have a tendency to think there are only certain situations in which bargaining is appropriate and effective. Do not make this mistake. Bargaining works at garage sales and flea markets as well as at car dealerships and vacation destinations. Remember; you won't get a good price if you do not ask for it.

My friend collects hand-blown glass figurines. He began his acquisitions in the service in Southeast Asia and has continued seeking new items for a collection for the last 30 years. They wanted a glass display case and began searching for one. We saw one in the reduced area of a large discount store. Even though it was reduced, we still had to bargain. It appeared to be missing the glass shelves and the bottom third was supposed to have a mirror, which was cracked. Well, we offered 25% less which was ½ the original price. When we got the cabinet to my house in a pick-up truck fully assembled, the glass shelves were taped to the underside of the bottom shelf.

Bargaining is not limited to physical items. Years ago, I had to retake a college course. I took a required science course I thought would be easy – geology. The teacher was remarkably boring, spoke in a monotone, and I ended up with an *F*. The second time around, I had to get at least a *B* in the class to pass. I had a different instructor, one who really loved his rocks! The class was fun, often humorous, and, therefore, easy to get a good grade in. When the grades were posted, I missed an *A* by just a few points. The grades were posted on the door of the professor's office and he was sitting inside. I shared with him my need to retake the class and how enjoyable he had made his subject. When I received my grades, the high *B* had become an *A*. The effort was not intentional, but shows that every situation can be advantageous if approached the right way.

Don't Be Picky

You are probably not going to get a great vacation bargain if you decide up-front on a week in Paris at a high-end hotel. However, my son is constantly jetting off at the last minute to foreign cities with discounted airfare and staying at picturesque inns at remarkably low prices. Off-season is also a great time to visit some vacation destinations.

Give the Seller a Reason to Negotiate

Assuring the local small retailer that you plan to become a regular customer, getting your car serviced at the dealer that gives you the good deal, and becoming a repeat customer at your favorite fresh vegetable stand can all provide the seller a reason for giving you their best price. Remember that all you need to do is make sure the seller gets some sort of a profit.

Ask Open-Ended Questions

Avoid questions that can be answered by a simple "yes" or "no," as they can stop negotiations cold. Start with a statement indicating your need for an item and ending with a request for a response. Here are some examples:

- "We just bought a new house and need quite a bit of new furniture. What is the best way to accomplish this?"

- "Our daughter needs a reliable car because she is going to college out of state. We are not sure if we should buy an inexpensive new car or a reliable used car. What would you suggest?"

You can also use the following phrases in your open-ended questions to get negotiation started:

- How can you help me?

- What is the best option for me?

- What would you suggest we do?

Display Your Knowledge

You will gain the respect of the individual with whom you are negotiating if you show you know something about the product. Doing so shows the seller you share their passion and indicates you are a qualified buyer. If you are not an expert, do your research before bargaining so you have a basic knowledge of the product. Showing respect for the product and the seller's love of it goes a long way in building the rapport necessary to get a good bargain.

Be Discreet

Some sellers may not want to make your great deal public. This is especially true in salary negotiations. Letting your new co-workers know the great salary you have is not the way to bond with your new fellow employees. In addition, sometimes the bargain you get is so great, the seller simply cannot provide it more than once. Sharing your good fortune can create an uncomfortable situation for the seller and close the door for future positive bargaining outcomes.

Bargaining in Specific Situations

Negotiating Salary

When you either negotiate salary, for a new position or as part of a promotion, begin by knowing what you are worth. Ask yourself the following questions before you begin:

- Is what you are bringing to the job hard to come by?

- How much are you and your skills worth?

- What edge do you bring to the negotiation?

Never Feel Rushed

Sometimes your ability to successfully negotiate and get what you want is simply outlasting the other person. Be patient, as what frequently happens in negotiating is that one or both individuals get tired and are ready to accept an offer they would not ordinarily accept because they are tired. You are more likely to get what you want if you can outlast the other person.

Make a Plan

Decide before negotiation begins how you will structure your proposal – what you plan to offer the other person. A salary negotiation is a series of exchanges – one person offers a proposal and the other person counter-proposes. The structure of your proposal can lead to either success or disaster.

When negotiating a starting salary, start asking for more than you expect. You may have a pleasant surprise and get agreement immediately. If not, the other person is less likely to go too low, or they will feel like they are taking advantage of you.

Don't worry about insulting them by making an offer they may consider too low or high. If they do not like your offer, they can always counter. Be bold, but respectful. Be prepared to explain why you have chosen that amount – previous job experience, the duties of the job, cost of living, your educational edge, etc. Research how much people in equivalent positions are paid in your area, print out those statistics, and take them with you.

Purchasing Food

One big-ticket item for many families is food. Maybe it is because food is considered a necessity, but most people do not consider food to be an item open for negotiation. However, just as with any other items, foodstuffs are also obtainable at bargain prices. Outdoor and roadside markets are good places to put your bargaining skills at work. Frequently, growers will be willing to offer a discount for a bulk sale, so you may wish to consider freezing or canning veggies like tomatoes or green beans.

Even grocery retailers are open to granting bargains for selling older or overstocked items. This is an area where the rule of, "You don't get anything you don't ask for," applies. Look for bargains in perishable items such as dairy products, bread, meat, and vegetables. Watch sell-by dates and offer to purchase expiring items at a reduced price.

Mail Order

Frequently, mail order companies offer discounts based upon the amount of an order. Another possible discount you can request is on shipping. Sometimes the item you buy is less expensive than the shipping fees. My son always asks for free shipping and gets it about half the time.

My spouse does a great deal of EBay shopping. A number of times, an offer was made for multiple items at a discount from a seller with several different items listed. By doing so, we saved as much as 15%.

Insurance

Progressive Insurance uses bargaining as a sales tool. They offer the prices of their competitor to get you to purchase their insurance. You can use the same method. When it is time to renew your insurance, do some shopping for lower prices. If you find one, tell your agent what you found and that you are considering changing insurance companies. More than likely, you will get a competitive quote.

Additionally, make sure you review your insurance coverage each year. You many no longer want comprehensive and collision coverage on an older vehicle you recently paid off. Check with agent about combining insurance plans, such as your home and auto insurance. Ask if there are discounts for driver courses, offered by some states.

Conclusion

Now that you have learned the steps necessary for successful negotiation, actively seek opportunities to apply what you have learned. Begin by recognizing that people often ask for more than they expect to get. Don't be apologetic in your approach, but remember that the seller is asking a price that covers their costs and still provides a profit. As such, they have room to negotiate. Conditioning yourself to negotiate at every opportunity will help you become more comfortable, confident and successful.

When you negotiate, be pleasant and persistent, but not demanding. So much of successful negotiation is depending upon having the proper attitude. My children are naturals with this skill. Eldest son makes friends wherever he goes and makes repeat visits to foreign destinations, cultivating friendships that provide a personal interaction with the people and their culture. Youngest son is loved and remembered by everyone and gets good deals based upon simple asking. Daughter learned from her Dad to bargain on everything! Additionally, she looks for scratches, dents, and missing parts that can serve her well in the negotiation process.

Bargaining is very personal and as you hone your skills, you will develop a "bargaining personality" unique and special. You will become comfortable with the process of bargaining. Not only will you save money, but also you will set up win-win situations where both you and the other party involved in the negotiation come away from the deal feeling happy and successful.

So, get busy and bargain. The rewards are great – both personally and monetarily.

Final Negotiation Tips

Negotiation, bargaining, or haggling, there are certain simple steps that can make the process easy and fun.

- Try to remember to have your starting price a little less than half of the original price.

- Always be reasonable, respectful, and polite with the seller.

- Be aware of your body language as a skilled bargainer will pick up on non-verbal signals that give away your true feelings.

- Be firm in your language and your proposals, using "I" statements.

- Conceal your emotions as much as possible, especially if the seller surprises you with a very appealing offer you didn't expect.

- Remember that preparation is 90% of negotiation, so gather as much information as you can, evaluate all the key variables, and know what concessions you are willing to make.

- Listen carefully and build on your gathered information as you negotiate.

- Speak with authority, in a rather loud, clear voice to give the impression that you have done this many times before and have experience getting good bargains.

- Take the lead in conversations about price, because if they mention a price, they subconsciously validate what they say and it is hard to move them from the price they have stated.

- Keep the conversation positive and upbeat, as hostility or a bad mood can kill a deal.

- If possible, bargain up in price, starting with the lowest price you are willing to pay and then work your way up until you both agree.

www.ingramcontent.com/pod-product-compliance
Lightning Source LLC
Chambersburg PA
CBHW070749180526
45168CB00004B/1573